Wendy Chibesakunda

THE LEGAL COURT v THE COURT OF PUBLIC OPINION

Wendy Chibesakunda

THE LEGAL COURT v THE COURT OF PUBLIC OPINION

The growth of Internet Jurisdiction and the importance of Private International Law

Dictus Publishing

Cover image: www.ingimage.com

Publisher:
Dictus Publishing
is a trademark of
Dodo Books Indian Ocean Ltd. and OmniScriptum S.R.L publishing group

120 High Road, East Finchley, London, N2 9ED, United Kingdom
Str. Armeneasca 28/1, office 1, Chisinau MD-2012, Republic of Moldova, Europe
Printed at: see last page
ISBN: 978-613-7-35687-6

THE LEGAL COURT

V

THE COURT OF PUBLIC OPINION

The growth of Internet Jurisdiction and the Importance of Private International Law

A Book by Wendy Chibesakunda

DEDICATION

To my parents, I know you are extremely proud of me.

There is nothing like a Public Slaughter

Background

The Court of Public Opinion has been in existence through the ages in the form of mob justice, personal vendettas and public fixing. Not usually legally constituted, but highly effective for those seeking instant "justice" in the eyes of the privileged beholder. The attack is obviously on the reputation of the other party, but concern must be brought to the legal repercussions that may occur because the statute of limitation is not a concern and neither is locus standi or even the rules, conventions, models law of Private International Law.

A lot of understanding is needed to change the mindset of those who are quick to play the role of Prosecutor, Judge, Jury and Executioner, sometimes without the full facts or even following the rules of natural justice that are in place for good reason. The law acts as an authority for social habits and patterns of behavior that are generally acceptable in many jurisdictions and the first source to be looked at, is the national law and from there, other legal systems are acknowledged and highly regarded to be harmonized in one form or another to resolve problems or methods that may arise.

Defences are relied upon to exonerate or exculpate a victim or an accused person, this is where the issue of control is also reserved for the court in the course of proceedings and the Court of Public Opinion can be greatly questioned if it is empowered or indeed entitled to take away the right of a person to defend himself. Points of law and fact are essential for an effective legal decision that can act as a precedent and administration of Justice. The issue of an appeal on grounds of law and fact is also very cardinal.

TABLE OF CONTENTS

ABBREVIATIONS

ARIPO African Regional Intellectual Property Rights

CIDIP Conferencia de Derecho Internacional Provido

CLIP Conflict of Laws in Intellectual Property

EAPO European Patent Organization

EPO European Patent Office

EU European Union

GCCI Global Chamber of Commerce and Industry

GDDS General Data Dissemination System

HCCH Hague Conference on Private International Law

HIPAA Health Insurance Portability and Accountability

ISO International Organization for Standadization

ICSID International Center for Settlement of Disputes

IMF International Monetary Fund

MIGA Multilateral Investment Guarantee Agency

OAPI Organization Africaine de la Propriete

PCI Payment Card Industry

PCT International Patent System

SOC Security Operations Center

TRIPS Trade Related Aspects of Intellectual Property

UNCITRAL United Nations Commission on International Trade Law

UNIDROIT International Institute for the Unification of Private Law

UNTOC United Nations Convention against Transnational Organized Crime

WIPO World Intellectual Property Organization

WTO World Trade Organization

CHAPTER ONE

INTERNET JURISDICTION

This is an issue that is very complex and has taken many years to address and very few issues have been resolved because of the highly complex digital ecosystem, but the bigger issue is harmonization and development capacity within a national context meaning that many countries have unilateral measures, but common rules always help.

Data Governance according to the World Bank leads to improved development outcomes, improved poverty mapping which can lead to improvements in targeting and service delivery. If Data Governance is that important, then when it comes to Mobile technologies leveraging off DATA, particularly smartphones, have the potential to bring about development, but identified policies that need to be put in place include:

- An integrated national data system (INDS) which call for INDS that allows the flow of data among a wide array of users in a way that facilitates safe use and reuse of data.
- Developing a new social contract for data based on the pillars of trust, equity, and value.
- Collaborate to accelerate developmental objectives and data literacy with government structures that deal with research and development for technology.
- The Data culture must be constantly monitored.

The issue of territory and jurisdiction in Private International Law can never be down played especially when the importance of Private Data is very much regarded as of high importance.

- The Organization of Economic Cooperation and Development (OECD) promotes the respect of private data and the flow of information by providing a uniform forum of evidenced based policy analysis with the privacy guidelines in place for minimum standards and data protection.
- Special Jurisdiction Provisions determine the competence of the national laws and data protection authorities in areas of permissions and prohibitions; and many countries have adopted general data protection and privacy laws for control and supervision purposes.

When the internet acts as a free vehicle for the transmission of messages, and leaking of information, it can act as Judge, Jury and Prosecutor with relentless headlines and news which can be true or false, but can lead to harmful consequences of strangers accosting you with no remorse.

The European Union has put data protection under public scrutiny to provide security and empowerment and it does not matter where a citizen of the EU is located, privileges are recognized and the silos mentality is very much contained or almost erased with transparency is key and compliance is the order, a lack of transparency may lead to levy fines under the General Data Protection Regulation from May 25, 2018.

Canada has similar provisions as the GDPR, Japan has not been left behind in collecting and managing personal data and Brazil from 2020 has a well regulated system for data protection similar to Europe, Most Asian countries have kept up with new legislation and the State of California has had private data regulation to protect consumer privacy since 1998.

This is the era of Big Data, data protection and private rights and Privacy is generally accepted as a Human Right worldwide and the access and storage of data is a daily concern as the digital ecosystem continually undergoes changes.

The **Lisbon Treaty** brought the unification of the **EU** and political unions were upheld, with the creation of the European Parliament which brought a lot of unification in regulation of currency, trade and many other fields.

Convention 108 of the EU (1981) is The Convention for the Protection Of Individuals with regard to Automatic Processing of personal data, due recognition is given that it was the first Data Protection international instrument, still legally binding and other related laws or protocols have emerged for instance, in 2019 Guidelines on Artificial intelligence and Data protection.

The transmission of information is done by a sequence of data that is received after it has been communicated and transmission of data is closely related to Information Management which deals with guidelines and policies that deal with regulation, risk management and accessibility.

The issue of security eventually arises because the requirement of freedom from risk or harm of a person, assets or property is very important, an environment of safety that creates that security, reduces harm which can be unintentional or accidental or even deliberate. Information Management incidences will be contained by: reporting, recording, analyzing, information sharing, decision making, trends and patterns, risk assessment and management, this will lead to the strategic decision. Legally and ethically, confidentiality is very important and data security is often implemented physically, digitally, by backups, destruction of data and communication security. The duty of care never ceases in information management especially where there is procedure, guidelines and professionalism. Law Enforcement Agencies have to be informed in the prescribed manner and the media should be advised sparingly and accordingly to avoid alarming a situation if the security of a person or nation is in issue. Monitoring of information, social media, publications, FAQ (Frequently asked Questions) answers and all data transmission will control the flow of information.

Cyber Security

The security will take the form of Advance threat protection, Network Security, Data Security, Mobile Security Application Security, Infrastructure Security, System security and importantly the aspect of Risk Governance and Compliance which for purposes of regulation considers:

- Audit and Compliance Analysis
- Configuration Compliance
- Firewall Compliance and Management
- ISO 27001
- HIPAA
- PCI
- SOC

The above factors and below treaties are helpful in Cyber Security for purposes of control and compliance.

When it comes to cyber security it has been identified as essential for innovation, connectivity and freedom of expression. Dealing with effective management is highly considered as a control method with the help of Treaties such as:

United Nations Convention against Transnational Organised Crime ('UNTOC') The Convention is further supplemented by three Protocols, which target specific areas and manifestations of organized crime: the Protocol to Prevent, Suppress and Punish Trafficking in Persons, Especially Women and

Children; the Protocol against the Smuggling of Migrants by Land, Sea and Air; and the Protocol against the Illicit Manufacturing of and Trafficking in Firearms, their Parts and Components and Ammunition. Countries must become parties to the Convention itself before they can become parties to any of the Protocols.

Signed on the 23 November 2001 and entered into force on 1 July 2004The Council of Europe's Convention on Cybercrime ('Convention') was the first multilateral binding instrument to regulate cybercrime and addressed the issue of elimination of safe havens, cooperation between law enforcement agencies and the address of fundamental rights in different legal systems which mainly address criminalization. The Convention addressed offences against the confidentiality, integrity and availability of computer data and systems; computer-related offences (computer-related fraud and forgery); content-related offences child pornography and criminal copyright infringement without addressing cyber terrorism, spam or identity theft. Criminal offences are not tried in absentia

World Summit on the Information Society, held in Geneva in 2003 has the following action lines:

- Cooperation among stakeholders
- Millennium Declaration
- Mainstreaming ICTs
- Multi Stakeholder Partnership (MSP) •
- Multi-stakeholder portals for indigenous peoples
- National e-strategies
- Public/Private Partnerships (PPP).

The birth of the Geneva Declaration of Principles and the Geneva Plan of Action the objectives of the Plan of Action came forth to build an inclusive Information

Society; to put the potential of knowledge and ICTs at the service of development; to promote the use of information and knowledge for the achievement of internationally agreed development goals. The Geneva Convention prohibits murder, mutilation, torture, the taking of hostages, unfair trial, and cruel, humiliating and degrading treatment.

2007 the International Telecommunication Union (ITU), which is responsible for facilitating action line C5, launched its Global Cyber security Agenda (GCA) ITU is an accredited training center for EC-Council, the world's largest cyber security technical certification body. The mission of EC-Council is to provide information security training that will ultimately help guard against a devastating cyber - attacks. The ITU sets and publishes regulations and standards relevant to electronic communication and broadcasting technologies of all kinds including radio, television, satellite, telephone and the Internet.

In Salvador, Brazil, from 12 to 19 April 2010, the Twelfth United Nations Congress on Crime Prevention and Criminal Justice was held. The following Declaration was made:

1. The recognition of an effective, fair and humane criminal justice system is based on the commitment to uphold the protection of human rights in the administration of justice and the prevention and control of crime.
2. The recognition that it is the responsibility of each Member State to update, where appropriate, and maintain an effective, fair, accountable and humane crime prevention and criminal justice system.
3. The value and impact of the United Nations standards and norms was acknowledged in crime prevention and criminal justice, so as to use those

standards and norms as guiding principles in designing and implementing national crime prevention and criminal justice policies, laws, procedures and programmes.

4. Bearing in mind the universal character of the United Nations standards and norms in crime prevention and criminal justice, an invitation to the Commission on Crime Prevention and Criminal Justice was made, to consider reviewing and, if necessary, updating and supplementing them. In order to render them effective, we recommend that appropriate efforts be made to promote the widest application of those standards and norms and to raise awareness of them among authorities and entities responsible for their application at the national level.
5. The need for Member States to ensure effective gender equality in crime prevention, access to justice and the protection offered by the criminal justice system was highly acknowledge.

This brought a lot of mixed feelings and experts groups convened in 2011 and 2012.

2013 produced the Directive on Attacks against Information Systems where offences and penalties were clearly outlined.

2016 the Directive on Security Network and Information Systems in the European Union came into force.

The EU Cyber Resilience Act came into force in 2019 and introduced the voluntary certification scheme for products, services and processes. The Cyber Security risks continued and in 2022 it was observed that internet users were victim to baby monitors, robo vacuum cleaners, wi-fi routers and alarm systems and the act is there to impose Cyber Security obligations by default principles and imposes a duty of care for the life cycle of the products.

In 2011 Australia, July 11-14. Law Ministers and Attorneys-General from 44 countries attended, and the Meeting addressed many challenging issues currently faced by member states, including cybercrime enacted the Commonwealth Model Law on Computer and Computer Related Crimes. The Ministers resolved on cybercrime as follows:

- to recognise the significant threat cybercrime poses to national security and law enforcement in all countries of the Commonwealth;
- that the Commonwealth Secretariat form a multidisciplinary working group of experts to review the practical implications of cybercrime in the Commonwealth and identify the most effective means of international co-operation and enforcement, taking into account, amongst others, the Council of Europe Convention on Cybercrime, without duplicating the work of other international bodies; and
- that the Working Group collaborate with other international and regional bodies with a view to identifying best practice, educational material and training programmes for investigators, prosecutors and judicial officers.

In 2010 The Arab Convention on Combating Information Technology Offences was enacted with the aim of enhancing cooperation between Arab countries 'to combat information technology offences threatening their security, interests and the safety of their communities' this was to help the Arab world to predict the future and respond to variables. The different and differentiated situations of the Arab States with regard to the adoption of a national strategy for cybersecurity and related legislations have not prevented the emergence of a number of initiatives for the joint Arab action. The Arab Convention aimed to:

- To counter offences that adopt information technologies as information technology offences and to establish a framework for the investigation and prosecution of such offences. The following acts were identified in the list of technical offences.
- Counter illicit access to, presence in or contact with part or all of the information technology, or the perpetuation thereof. •
- Counter the deliberate unlawful interception of the movement of data by any technical means, and the disruption of transmission or reception of information technology data.
- Counter the offence Against the Integrity of Data - Deliberate unlawful destruction, obliteration, obstruction, modification or concealment of information technology data.

In the area of protection of personal data, some Arab States have established national bodies to monitor personal data, a procedural legal system for its tracing, a special regulatory and oversight body, a legal regime for international cooperation and a framework for internal cooperation between the cybersecurity system components.

In 2011 An African Union Convention on Cyber Security and Personal Data Protection was drafted to establish a 'credible framework for cybersecurity in Africa through organization of electronic transactions, protection of personal data, promotion of cyber security, e-governance and combating cybercrime. The Malabo Convention envisions Africa as a single entity in terms of data and privacy protection and calls for a harmonized, independent, and robust legal framework which protects all people from processors and data controllers. Considering that the goal of this Convention is to address the need for harmonized legislation in the area of cyber security in Member States of the African. Despite all the great policies and regulations the Malabo Convention promises to deliver, the Convention still hasn't taken effect, as only 2 states of the 55 member states have ratified the convention.

Electronic Communication

Many challenges arise in electronic communication, but risk in real time and security needs to connect users to Digital Trust expectancy is on the part of every person that values are upheld by giving due regard to privacy issues, mitigation and retention. This is highly connected to Data Protection Law which deals with control, security, privacy and the ultimate value.

Data Protection Law

The European Union's General Data Protection Regulation has been recognized as the ideal one to upgrade a uniform global environment on data protection and privacy rights, although it must be added that many other countries across the globe are developing standards to keep up with the constantly changing digital world.

Competition Law

In 1980, the United Nations Conference on Restrictive Business Practices approved the **Set of Multilaterally Agreed Equitable Principles and Rules for the Control of Restrictive Business Practices (The UN Set)** for adoption as a resolution, which are added every five years and UNCTAD always plays a major role..

The UN Set is a multilateral agreement on competition policy that:

- Provides a set of equitable rules for the control of anti-competitive practices.
- Recognizes the development dimension of competition law and policy.
- Provides a framework for international operation and exchange of best practices.

This framework also provides vital technical assistance and capacity-building for interested member States so that they are better equipped to use competition law and policy for development.

The creation of more sector-specific competition provisions in the WTO, such as in the Basic Telecommunications Agreement, might lead to inconsistent competition policies across sectors. The international dispute settlement process is easier when the binding agreements are uniform, but this proves problematic to the fact based Anti-Trust Cases which are generally described as complex.

The best approach is by looking at:

- Core Principles,
- Common Approaches.

Standards must never be compromised for the sake of advocacy, investigation and regulation.

Transaction Law

With respect to substantive provisions, the Electronic Communications Convention builds extensively, on the fundamental principles of the uniform law of electronic commerce developed by UNCITRAL (non-discrimination, technological neutrality, functional equivalence, and irrelevance of place of origin) it removes obstacles arising from formal requirements contained in other international trade law treaties; 2) it provides a common substantive core to the law of electronic communications, thus ensuring a higher level of uniformity both in the legislative text and in its interpretation; 3) it updates and complements the provisions of the MLEC and of the MLES; 4) it provides core legislation on electronic communications to those States not having yet any, or having partial and insufficient provisions.

The United Nations Convention on Contracts for the International Sale of Goods (CISG). Therefore, the ECC applies if the law the law of a State party to the European Economic Community ECC, or if the parties have validly chosen as the law applicable to their communications or the application of the substantive provisions of the ECC if chosen by virtue of agreement of the parties.

The political, media, and technological factors are very significant for the sake of public awareness in the generation of press releases for the image building of the Judiciary and to show that the wheels of Justice although slow, are still turning. The Judiciary is still an authority figure and controls many aspects of society and the powers of Adjudication fall within the systems of the Court, but Tribunals may have Judicial powers or quasi- Judicial powers, meaning that, they are closely related to the executive and entrusted to determine facts according to the dictates of policy, the Tribunals with Judicial powers will determine both the law and facts and decide according to the law, the powers of Tribunals can both be administrative or judicial by nature.

The one true fact is that the Court of Public Opinion is mostly full of allegations from people without any legal standing and sometimes no due regard to the value of evidence or national regulation, but basically holds a narrative of facts and sometimes lies only to the knowledge of the author. The fact is, reputation once destroyed, can never be recovered. The Court of Public Opinion is usually a dangerous ground and the possibility of allegations leading to actual litigation are very high.

The Middle East and Asia censors internet use quite openly, the other forms of regulation are Laws as is the basic theme, Architecture which is generally mentioned, Norms are briefly explained, and Markets. Internet regulation is a complex and covers many sectors which are sector-specific and medium-specific laws.

New research has shown that collecting personal data, tracking, and scale profiling has affected security, data protection rights, democracy and the environment and the EU regulatory framework has been highly acclaimed.

REFERENCES:

1. Oren Bigos (2005) Jurisdiction on Cross border wrongs on the internet, Oxford Press.
2. Jonathan Clough ( ) A world of difference: the budapest convention on cybercrime and the challenges of harmonization.
3. The Arab Cyber Security Vision. Businessnews.com
4. www.europarl.europa.eu/thinktank

CHAPTER TWO

JUDICIAL AUTHORITY, JUDICIAL FUNCTIONS, COMPETENCE, PERSONAL JURISDICTION AND JUDICIAL FORUM

The court of Public Opinion is sometimes more influential and controversial than the court of law since the audience is large, sometimes merciless without fully understanding the legal implications involved. The Court of Public Opinion more often than not, attacks the reputation of the person or personality that is involved and that is why big corporations will have a department or hire expert trackers of any or all internet related attacks that can lead to potential scandals. The media is always used and it influences every medium that will have a positive or negative effect and the outcome can potentially injure the reputation of the party involved by the free expression of opinions, especially in a democracy.

Freedom of expression

The Court is a place that is usually perceived to be impartial, it has the controls and methods of coordination through jurisdiction and the law. Except in as far as Treason, blasphemy, blackmail, sedition, obscenity, perjury and defamation are considered as contravention of the law, a person may express their views as prescribed. The limitation is limited if an unlawful act is committed, the necessary measures will be taken to control the situation. In a 'State of Emergency' situation, the government will act with more powers and individual rights are sometimes completely controlled by the government for the safety of the entire nation or public necessity and maintenance of sovereign powers, but such acts must be done in good faith.

To avoid the heavy cost of legal proceedings, or the imputation of alignment to defamation, many wisely seek legal advice before saying, writing or publishing anything that may result in any form of legal proceedings, others as a safety measure prefer not to issue any comments or statements.

Suffice to say, with technology, many issues of internet jurisdiction have arisen, which have no or very few legal precedents and the issues often vary.

***Google Inc v Equustek Solutions Inc* [2017] 1 SCR 824** , [41] the Supreme Court of Canada recently observed that ' the natural habitat of the internet is global and private international law doctrines provide a key part of the legal background against which much advice to clients seeking to have any kind of Internet presence must be framed.

The Supreme Court of Canada granted an interlocutory injunction against Google to remove all of a company's websites from its worldwide search engineThe injunction was ordered in the interest of justice with the Supreme Court of Canada finding that de-indexing the defendant's domain from Google's search engine globally was necessary to prevent irreparable harm to Equustek. The Supreme Court was unconvinced by Google's arguments that a global de-indexing order would offend international comity, would unreasonably inconvenience the search engine, and would interfere with the right to freedom of expression. The U.S. District Court of Northern California granted Google a temporary injunction blocking the enforceability of the Supreme Court of Canada's order in the U.S. The California Court granted the injunction on the basis that the company was protected as a neutral intermediary under Section 230 of the Communications Decency Act 1996. Held: This judgment contracts freedom of expression by banning results from a search engine on a worldwide scale. In this case, the allegations against the defendant were flagrant and the impugned websites amounted to commercial speech (which is afforded more limited protection under international law).

Internet Jurisdiction over the website operator

The degree of internet presence plays an important role in management and control of information and a "passively accessible" website is insufficient to sustain general jurisdiction as opposed to the limitation to define the parameters of personal jurisdiction in the Internet context, specifically for passive websites that only advertise local services.

Bensusan Restaurant Corp. v. King Bensusan Restaurant Corporation ("Bensusan") was a New York corporation that owned "The Blue Note," a jazz club in Greenwich Village, New York. Bensusan owned all trademark rights, title and interest in the federally registered "The Blue Note" mark. Richard B. King was a Missouri resident who owned "The Blue Note" club in Columbia, Missouri and he advertised the club in 1996 based on information about the club in Missouri as well as a calendar of events and ticketing information, that did not go well with Bensusan Restaurant who decided to sue for trade mark infringement, , trademark dilution and unfair competition. On the other hand, King moved to dismiss the action for lack of personal jurisdiction pursuant to Federal Rules of Civil Procedure

Held: that defendant Richard B. King's Internet website did not satisfy New York's long-arm statute requirements for plaintiff Bensusan Restaurant Corporation to bring a trademark infringement suit in New York. The District Court's decision also likened creating a website to merely placing a product into the stream of commerce, and held that such an act was insufficient to satisfy due process and personal jurisdiction requirements.

Some people sometimes feel the need to win in the Court of Public Opinion and that is why their defense in a Court of law is very important and once their names are cleared, the Court of Public opinion also goes viral in clearing their names and the once tainted reputation is cleared because of the public shaming and injustice. The effect of internet numbers on the side can highly glamorize a picture that is not true and hence the person or personality upheld shows some levels of control. The interim relief or preliminary relief still lies in the real court room and not on the internet where any statement you say will definitely be used online and the result can lead on the negative path of business closing, career destruction and possibly many cover ups.

Previously for an action to be entertained in an English Court for a wrong to be justiciable it had to be actionable in an English Court and that being said, Private International Law has paved the way and changed many legal requirements with model laws and legal principles such as: the validity of the action, the character of the wrong committed, the legal standing of the parties and the law of the forum, from there the foreign elements that can be entertained; international conventions, protocols and rules have eased the way for many legal proceedings and /or alternative dispute resolution.

Coca Cola Co v All-Fect Distributing Co [1999] FCA 1721.

The contour drawing mark was highlighted in issue and the trade mark. The trade mark is registered in class 32 in respect of beverages and syrups for the manufacture of such beverages. At first instance two other registered trade marks were in issue – the word marks “Coca-Cola” and “Coke”. The Respondent was a wholesaler and had a cola flavoured confectionary which is shaped somewhat like the contour bottle. The appellant contended that the extensive use, including the licensing, of the contour bottle as a trade mark has resulted in the bottle being so well known in Australia that it is understood by the public to be used exclusively in connection with products made by, for, or with the approval of the appellant. Held: The appeal must be allowed. In lieu of the orders made by the primary judge it should be ordered that the matter be remitted to him for further consideration of the "defence" under s 120(2) and the claims under the *Trade Practices Act* and for passing off. The respondent should pay the appellant's costs of the appeal. Since the matter is to be remitted, we would leave to the primary judge the question of the costs of the trial and the proceedings on the remitter.

The fact that there are many legal systems with different values, history and tradition has affected the development of law, legal systems and sometimes public opinion over time.

A typical case that materializes in the Court of Public opinion is:

The Duke of Lacrosse Case

Three players were charged with rape in a case that became a national scandal, impacted by issues of race, politics and class. In April 2007, all charges against the young men were dropped due to lack of credible evidence and the district attorney was eventually disbarred for his mishandling of the case. In the end, there was no trial—a fact that most people forget. The three players received **$20 million each** in a settlement with Duke. The university spent more than $100 million between legal fees, settlement costs, and other expenses to move on from the ignominy and preserve its "brand."

10 years later ESPN felt the need to make a documentary about the whole incident and all parties were invited to tell their side of the story in their 30 for 30 series,

none of the true parties named in the case appeared, but their families expressed their views and sentiments.

Private international law has no universal definition but starts from national courts which have laws, rules and regulations as well a principles that will determine any conflict in laws by looking at nationality, the transactions, forum, the place of property and the place of the transaction. The treaties that a country has and will sign have a great impact on the harmonization and development of Private International Law.

Jurisprudential, substantive and procedural,

The Jurisprudence of Private International law deals with international contracts, torts, family law, child adoption and abduction, real property, intellectual property and the recognition of foreign judgments, this recognizes that every sovereign nation, the legal systems. The institutions and the different societies that will the private international law will apply to are also taken into account. In Jurisprudence the theories that are basically considered stem from Statutes, International Theories, Territories, National laws and the Justice Systems.

The Substantive Part of private International Law are basically the rules that apply in Constitutions, Common Law. Treaties, Protocols, Model laws and other recognized guidelines for the purpose of regulation.

The Procedural Part of Private International law are the rules of the Court, the remedies that will enforce rights and duties by providing redress.

Judicial Authority

Legislative Authority and Judicial Authority have been described as two powers that move together to measure the strength and weaknesses of an exercising power because the Court has to decide on the issue of Jurisdiction. If it is a contract issue, then the National provisions and the laws that will apply provided that the contract is valid, the Tort has occurred in the jurisdiction or the Administrative action occurred in that jurisdiction

Judicial functions and Competence:

The ability of the Court to decide the law and resolve disputes is the function and the rules of natural justice must apply to protect all parties and the record of proceedings must be available to show the legal status; and the ability of the Court to exercise its Jurisdiction is competence that is expressed through adjudication and decision making.

Personal Jurisdiction of the Court:

Recognizing that Jurisdiction may come through territory, resolving security risks and basic human rights, Jurisdiction most times is distinguished to ease the due process of the law which in turn limits the exercise of jurisdiction.

The personal Jurisdiction of the Court is limited by the Constitution to the persons and proper within its jurisdiction, provided that it is a valid action. If the Court is not bound by any international instruments, then the National laws will apply to ensure the protection of the citizens and to fully implement their own laws in spite of the rules of natural justice; the domicile of the Defendant may be considered, but if bound by International Instruments, then the Jurisdiction according to the instrument in question will apply and the Defendant will need to avail himself.

The choice of court will be decided and the domicile or resident or habitual residence of the Defendant may not be an issue relevant to the proceedings.

Common Law countries personal jurisdiction means that the court has jurisdiction over a defendant in a personal action in the United Kingdom, USA, the Commonwealth in Africa and common law jurisdictions of Australia, parts of Canada, Hong Kong SAR, Singapore and New Zealand. Service is required even if the defendant is domiciled in the forum. In Common law countries, even if a court is competent to hear a dispute, it may nevertheless decline to hear it on the basis that it is clearly an inappropriate forum

Then there is Canada which is bi jural and recognizes the Quebec Civil Law and Common Law

Exceptions: are based on foreign property, diplomatic immunity and foreign state immunity

European Union allows personal jurisdiction in tort cases in the place where the event in relevant to the issue occurs

Subject Matter Jurisdiction of the Court

The Brussels la Regulation in Article 4, jurisdiction may be based on **"general jurisdiction"** (the defendant's domicile), **"special jurisdiction"** (e.g., for matters relating to contract or tort) and **"exclusive jurisdiction"** (e.g.,for matters relating to validity of registered IP rights).

Brussels Convention, art. 21: "*When proceedings involving the same cause of action and between the same parties are brought in Courts of different Contracting States, any Court other than the Court first seised shall of its own motion decline jurisdiction in favour of that Court.*"

The Brussels Convention does not apply where the judgment to be enforced was not from a Convention party. Generally, these rules apply only to defendants domiciled in another Member State, not to defendants domiciled in a non-Member State. These are rules laid down by the legislature of all the Member States of the Brussels Convention and its Parliament and Council.

Laguna Convention (2007) Convention on Jurisdiction in Civil and Commercial Matters clarifies which national states have jurisdiction in civil and commercial disputes and Enforcement of Judgments. The EU has signed it on behalf of the members and the United Kingdom has acceded to it, while Denmark has an option to opt out.

The HCCH Service Convention

The HCCH Convention of 15 November 1965 on the Service Abroad of Judicial and Extrajudicial Documents in Civil or Commercial Matters is non mandatory, but applies exclusively.

The requirements are.

(i) The law of the forum State determines whether a document has to be transmitted abroad for service.

(ii) The address for the person.

(iii) For judicial or extrajudicial document

(iv) Only civil or commercial documents

The HCCH Convention of 18 March 1970 on the Taking of Evidence Abroad in Civil or Commercial Matters (the HCCH Evidence Convention) was concluded to establish methods of cooperation for taking evidence abroad in civil or commercial matters. Conscious that legal systems around the world vary as regards taking evidence, the Convention provides effective means to facilitate the cross-border transmission of requests to obtain evidence. Under the framework of the Convention, evidence can be taken (i) by means of Letters of Request, and (ii) by diplomatic or consular agents and commissioners. Evidence may be given by video conference and that evidence may be taken to another state, a letter of request is issued to take that evidence and the costs are borne by the parties.

The Convention on the service abroad of judicial and extrajudicial documents in civil and commercial matter came forth in 1969.
The 1980 Hague Convention on the Civil Aspects of International Child Abduction and the 1993 Hague Convention on Protection of Children and Co-operation in Respect of Inter-country Adoption.
In November 2007, the Hague Conference adopted a new multilateral instrument, the Convention on the International Recovery of Child Support and Other Forms of Family Maintenance, adopted in November 2007
The International law (Conferencia de Derecho Internacional Privado or CIDIP was first held in 1975. Over time, it has had conferences have taken place, leading to conventions, protocols, model laws and uniform documents.

Authenticated documents are done through: civil registry, ministry of justice, consular and ministry of foreign affairs of both state of origin and state of destination

Berne Convention in Article 5(2) the enjoyment and exercise of these rights shall not be subject to any formality; such enjoyment and such exercise shall be independent of the existence of the protection in the country of origin of the work.

World Intellectual Property Organization WIPO (1967)has governing bodies and procedures that have enabled the development of Intellectual Property over time for Industrial property and Copyright and related rights with issues like ownership, infringement and contractual obligations.

The Paris Convention for the Protection of Industrial Property in Articles 6 and 7 provides for the mutual independence of patents and trademarks, establishing that patents obtained for the same invention in multiple countries are independent of each other

Beijing Treaty on Audiovisual Performances (Article 5) performers shall enjoy the exclusive right of authorizing the making available to the public their performances fixed in audiovisuals in such a way that members of the public may access them from a place and time chosen by them.

WTO Agreement on Trade-related Aspects of Intellectual Property Rights (TRIPS Agreement

European Union Court of Justice

European Union Intellectual Property Office

EU Satellite Broadcasting and Cable Retransmission Directive…

African Regional Intellectual Property Organization ARIPO

African Intellectual Property Organization

Instruments facilitating the obtainment of a **bundle of rights** include the WIPO administered Patent Cooperation Treaty (PCT; patents), Madrid (trademarks), Hague (designs) and Lisbon (appellations of origin) Systems as well as regional instruments such as the Harare Protocol on Patents and Industrial Designs, the Banjul Protocol on Marks and the Arusha Protocol for the Protection of New Varieties of Plants administered by ARIPO, the European Patent Convention

(EPC) established in the framework of the European Patent Organization (EPO), and the Eurasian Patent Convention of the Eurasian Patent Organization (EAPO). Typically, once granted these rights are subject to national (or regional) laws and national (or regional) enforcement procedures.

Instruments granting **supranational, unitary IP rights** include those governing the European Union (EU) trademarks and Community design rights, the (future) unitary patent granted under the EPC, the Bangui Agreement administered by OAPI, and the Gulf Cooperation Council (GCC) patent system. These instruments may contain specific rules of jurisdiction establishing a separate and distinct court system, designating national courts with specific competences or relying on national courts to apply general private international law principles.

Some actions are enforced at **national level** only while others have **International jurisdiction** at specified courts others only entitle administrative actions.

The Hague counterparts are the1975 Inter-American Convention on Letters Rogatory and the 1975 Inter-American Convention on the Taking of Evidence Abroad (together with its additional protocol) serve similar functions.

The American Law Institute Intellectual Property Principles Governing Jurisdiction, Choice of Law, and Judgments in Transnational Disputes of 2008

European Max Planck Group's Principles on Conflict of Laws in Intellectual Property (CLIP) of 2011;

2008, UNCITRAL completed work on a new UN Convention on Contracts for the International Carriage of Goods Wholly or Partly by Sea. The Convention was adopted by the UN General Assembly on December 11, 2008.

The International Institute for the Unification of Private Law (known as UNIDROIT which has the following: the 1973 Convention on a Uniform Law on the Form of an International Will and a 1995 Convention on Stolen or Illegally Exported Cultural Objects. The Model laws on Franchise Disclosure (2002) and Leasing (2008). In 2004 Principles came forth, one on International Commercial Contracts and the other on Transnational Civil Procedure a joint collaboration with the American Law Institute. The 2001 Cape Town Convention on International Interests in Mobile Equipment, the 2006 Protocol addressing matters specific to aircraft and aircraft engines and the 2007 Protocol on 2007 the financing of railroad rolling stock (such as engines, freight cars, and passenger cars, 2009 UNIDROIT Convention on Substantive Rules for Intermediated Securities.

In efforts to build a stronger global Financial System to avoid spill- over effects of economic recession and the retreat of investors, a lot of reforms were made by the IMF, World Bank, the Bank of International Settlements, and the Basel Committee on Banking Supervision and market participants to strengthen the global financial sector internally and externally in terms of regulation. Standards, corporate governance, capital requirements and codes of good practice to limit moral hazards. The International Finance Corporation IFC promotes sector investment. There is also MIGA which promotes foreign direct investment and The International Centre for Settlement of Investment Disputes ICSID has conciliation or Arbitration for **foreign investors** and their hosts, all these measures harmonize dispute resolution methods.

The Special Data Dissemination Standards SDDS (1996) provided guidelines for members to have access to international capital markets and provide that information for economic and finance to the public.

The General Data Dissemination Standards (1997) for the members that are still developing statistical standards by providing a framework for data improvement.

Article IV of the International Monetary Fund

The IMF every year has bilateral discussions with member states and there is usually a free flow of information in relation to economies and financial information for economic development.

The Financial Stability Forum which is now the **Financial Stability Board** comprises authorities from Finance Ministries, Central Banks and international Finance bodies enhancing transparency in the financial sector, prudential oversight and effective risk management.

To address the growing number and diversity of business transactions which may sometimes culminate in disputes or misunderstanding, not to be left behind, October 28, 2010, the Standing Committee of the Eleventh National People's Congress adopted China's first statute on Conflicts Law Act. By April 1st 2011, Chinese law on private international law entered into force, with a prior history of frustration because of the anti- foreign attitudes previously entertained and methods of control of attitudes previously employed. Many reforms had to take place within and outside of China especially with the help of the Chinese in the diaspora. The Property Act in 2007, Tort Liability Act 2009 preceded the Conflict of Laws Act which came as a result of many conflicts in contract and Aviation and meant to resolve other civil disputes such as Property Law, Family Law, Torts, Contracts, Unjust Enrichment. In China, there are Mandatory Laws that cannot be derogated from no matter the foreign element and those have to be enshrined in all civil related relationships and these rules are in relation to Public Order and the Courts' Power to determine the applicable **SUBSTANTIVE LAW** according to the regulations for the purpose of promoting justice. .

In Australia, the Foreign Judgments Act 1991was under scrutiny (with its analogues in some 30 jurisdictions, excluding the United States and Mainland China but including Hong Kong SAR) displaces the common law in respect of judgments for a sum of money, other than taxes, fines or penalties

In New Zealand, service may be effected as of right "where any act or omission for or in respect of which damages are claimed was done or occurred in New Zealand"

In the United States of America, constitutional due process requirements inform courts' approaches to the exercise of personal jurisdiction statutes of the particular states in which they are situated. The Due Process Clause in the

Fourteenth Amendment to the Constitution of the United States and is a matter that is subjective to state law.

Article 25 of the ICSID Convention talks about Jurisdiction of the center,

(1) The Jurisdiction of the Centre shall extend to any dispute arising directly out of an investment. Between a contracting state or constituent sub division or agency of a Contracting State designated to the Centre by that State) and a national of another Contracting State, which the parties to the dispute consent in writing to submit to the Centre. When the parties have given their consent, no party may withdraw its consent unilaterally.

Important Considerations

1. The opportunity to bring the claim in a reasonable court;
2. The freedom to refuse to defend the claim in an unreasonable court.
3. If a court in a different country can legitimately hear the case without prejudice that should be highly considered.

Jurisdiction is granted to the Court upon personal service of Court proceedings on a natural person or service to the place of business of the legal personality. Where there are multiple defendants, the main defendant's domicile will generally bind the other defendants. All relevant circumstances are highly considered and Justice must not only be done, but must be seen to be done.

Locus standi

In China, the habitual residence of the Defendant will connect the forum of the law to be upheld as a connection for rights and actions except in (excluding the jural acts relating to family or succession for security reasons when the law of nationality shall apply.

In the United States, relationship between the claim and the defendant's activities in the state of the forum is highly considered.

Bangui Agreement specifies jurisdiction, stating that the owner of the patent has the right to institute legal proceedings before the court of the place of the infringement

Discretion of the Court

This is the power of the Judge to make a decision with the guidance of the law and this is a very powerful tool that is exercised under the law. The power of one to act to the dictates of own judgment with the guideline of the principles of the law. The fact that sometimes the procedures of law enforcement agencies are not clearly defined helps a Judge decide with discernment at law.

The discretion of the Court is usually seen for instance, at the point of sentencing where rehabilitation or deterrence is regarded by the Judge and that is sometimes referred to as Discretionary Justice. The degree of latitude is clearly noticed when a sentenced is pronounced from several options of what could be, at law.

In China, The Conflicts Act fails to provide any guiding principle where a tortious act and the ensuing damage occur in different places; consequently, judges are left with considerable discretion in selecting the applicable law.

Based on law The **Model Law on Secured Transactions** developed by the United Nations Commission on International Trade Law (UNCITRAL)provides different choice of law rules for the proprietary aspects of a security right in IP and for the contractual aspects. Article 99 of the Model Law provides that the law of the State in which the IP is protected governs the

Based on facts

The decision of the Court will be based according to the facts and circumstances because disputes arise from the different facts of the individuals that appear before Court and even the setting of damages is a Judicial fact discretion. The facts and the law that the facts apply to will be described in the decision. The grounds of appeal are always based on fact and law, it is extremely important for the Judges to find truth in the facts. Lawyers are regarded as friends of the Court and are supposed to present all facts relevant to the issues to the matters before Court, but of course, there is extreme bias inclined to their own clients and sometimes information may be withheld. In Criminal cases, the prosecutors are said to have the highest discretion.

Competence to deal with the case, this becomes an issue and the appropriate Court will handle the issue or transfer the proceedings for the appropriate court to handle their issue by Mandatory laws political, social or economic importance or significance to the public interest that they cannot be set aside despite the international nature of the dispute, which a Court can interpret.

Choice of Law: the choice of law may arise before any dispute occurs, at contractual level or during the formation of the contract and at the point when the dispute occurs; only that applicable law will arise not necessarily the legal issues especially in security issues relating to intellectual property law.

Equitable relief Common law and equitable causes of action are frequently invoked to supplement, or as alternatives to, statutory rights in this instance in a dispute a party may act or refrain from acting because legal remedies are not sufficient. An example of an Equitable relief is Compensation that is granted because of a loss and this is distinguished from monetary damages which are a legal relief.

Granting of Leave

This is basically permission granted from the Court according to the rules and procedures, a Motion or Application will be filed seeking permission and when you are granted leave, it means you have been given permission.

The **Brussels Regime** requires that any court other than the court first seized shall, of its own motion, stay its proceedings until the jurisdiction of the court first seized is established..

Recognition of Foreign Judgments

The rules established in an international or regional treaty, Common Law or by State law or statutes requiring the registration of judgments of certain countries and the Belgian Code on Private International Law where it applies. Conventions, Protocols in terms of territory to be regarded In the United Kingdom, special rules established in the Civil Jurisdictions and Judgments Act 1982 make provision for the recognition and enforcement of judgments and injunction as well as the

Brussels and Lugano Conventions. In the United States of America, enforcement of judgments is a matter of state law

The general Requirements for recognition of Foreign Judgements are:

1. The court of origin exercised "international jurisdiction,"

2. The decision was final and conclusive.

3. The decision was **on the merits**.

4., The **parties** must be **identical**, or privy to the foreign decision

The sums involved must be specified or fixed, otherwise the Court may refuse to enforce such Judgements.

When judgements are refused, the misapplication of ***lex fori*** is not a ground of refusal, but the following are the reasonable grounds for refusal:

1. If there is fraud involved.
2. Violation of the rules of natural justice.
3. No prior notice of proceedings.
4. The proceedings or judgment are contrary to public policy.
5. The matter in issue was already adjudicated on by a court of competent jurisdiction.
6. The Court lacked personal Jurisdiction.

The following Conventions and Protocols also provide conditions for their recognition and enforcement of foreign judgments in another Contracting State and the grounds for refusal.

The Montevideo Convention (1993) on the rights and duties of states amplified the need to defend integrity and independence of states for their conservation and prosperity and this was part of the declaration of statehood as part of customary international law.

Minsk Convention (1992) provides the rules of legal cooperation between member states in Civil, Criminal and Family matters. This ensures access to justice and the Convention has provisions on the service of court documents. If we consider the Russian Courts for example, if a decision is made in bankruptcy and insolvency, the Courts will refuse to enforce judgments based on the Minsk Convention and Kiev Convention. This also includes family law and especially alimony, state sovereignty, Intellectual Property, legal capacity, just to mention a few. There is also a list of alternatives that allow Judgments to be considered for refusal or recognition. Judicial acts of a preliminary nature are recognized in the convention.

The Las Leñas Protocol for dispute resolution in Civil, Commercial, Labour and Administrative matters this is a Protocol of cooperation and jurisdiction aid. Let us take the example of Brazil which is on recording as saying it has no reservations in the enforcement of treaties provided that there is a respect for public policy and national sovereignty as a party of this treaty into by Brazil, first approved by the National Congress and enacted by a presidential decree. The enforcement of foreign judgments in Brazil is based on: the Constitution, the Code of Civil Procedure and the Rules of Procedure of the Superior Court of Justice.

The Inter-American Convention on the Extraterritorial Validity of Foreign Judgments (1979) organizes American States on the regulation of foreign judgments

Arbitral Awards, the Arab League Judgments Convention

The role of the recognition and enforcement of foreign judgments as a tool of regional economic integration can be achieved by reforming national laws aligning with the internationally accepted standards. There is regional cooperation through multilateral instruments that guarantee and enforce foreign judgments.

Riyadh Convention (1983) over three decades of Arab cooperation in Judicial matters and the contracting states need to find a joint interpretation at all times the enforcement court must have evidence that the issuing jurisdiction enforces judgments reciprocally, has not contravened Sharia Law or Public Policy and this has to be confirmed by a Ministry of Justice.

The New York Convention recognized the Gulf Cooperation Council where states ratified the New York Convention, the potential challenges to the enforcement of a foreign arbitral award are consistent with international arbitration norms recognizing Sharia Law and Arab Public Policy

REFERENCES:

1. Dr. Annabelle Bennett and Mr. Sam Granata (2019) When Private International Law Meets Intellectual Property Law: A Guide for Judges WIPO HCC

2. Wendy Collins Perdue (2012) What's Sovereignty Got to Do with It?: Due Process, Personal Jurisdiction and the Supreme Court . Richmond School of Law Publications

3. Marcus Alexandre Matteucci Gomes and Fabiano Bruno Solano Pereira (2022)westlaw.com

4. Trevor C Hartley (2021) Basic Principles of Jurisdiction in Private International Law: The European Union, The United States and England. Cambridge University Press. Cambridge

5. Elina Izotkina (2021) Russian Federation signed Convention on the Recognition and Enforcement of Foreign Judgments in Civil or Commercial Matters. Lidings.com. Imperia Tower Moscow, Russia.

6. Zhengxin Huo (2011)Highlights of China's New Private International Law Act: From the Perspective of Comparative Law

7. (Eds) Michael Douglas, Vivienne Bath, Mary Keyes and Andrew Dickinson (2019)Commercial Issues in Private International Law:*A Common Law Perspective*. Hart. Oxford.

8. WIPO (2001) forum on private international law and intellectual property

9. Ukandedu,ac.uk

CHAPTER THREE

CONSEQUENTIALISM JURISPRUDENCE

The effect or consequence of an action has increasingly become the norm of many legal decisions that are based on consequentialism for the good of society as a whole. There are three areas of the law to be looked at: Civil, Criminal and administrative and in the same way, the related remedies are also addressed. The development of the Jurisprudence of Consequentialism ensures that there is no stray, but the selection of law is very clear and it becomes easier to predict and prescribe, helping to eliminate incompetency and indeterminacy. While national sovereignty still remains highly regarded in the determination of many outcomes, however, the application of the law may sometimes need guidance.

OAPI rights, while deriving from a uniform administrative system, are enforced in national civil and criminal courts which apply the legislation of each of the Member States in which they

Other forms of address would be Alternative Dispute Resolution through Arbitration, Mediation and Conciliation

The term ***'lex fori'*** literally means **a country applies its own local law** and **determines the jurisdiction.** *Lex fori* – the law of the forum. For this approach the court will apply its own national law to identify the legal issue. It should be noted that this approach is most commonly applied. *Pearce v Ove Arup Partnership Ltd* [1999] 1 All ER 769) Established that a plaintiff to establish that the alleged wrong was actionable according to the *lex fori* and not defensible according to the law of the place where the alleged wrong occurred.

In China, *lex fori* is highly recognized and all foreign-related relationships are governed by the law of forum

In the United Kingdom itself, the *lex fori* rule has been abolished by statute:

> Private International Law (Miscellaneous Provisions) Act 1995 (UK). In the United Kingdom, the passage of the 1995 Private International Law (Miscellaneous Provisions) Act means that the governing law is the *lex loci unless misplaced by the proper law of the tort.*

Lex causae – the law applicable to the substance. For this approach the judge will have to apply the actual body of law applicable to the legal question, which could be a foreign law. This approach implies a preliminary determination of the applicable law.

lex loci actus, and the civil relationship between the principal and the agent shall be governed by the law of the place where the agency relationship is established in China, the same is also true for (excluding the jural acts relating to family or succession), a natural person's civil conduct capacity shall be governed by the *lex loci actus*, provided that he/she has such capacity under that law, whereas he/she lacks it under the law of his habitual residence.

lex loci celebrationis

Article 21 of the Conflict of laws Act in China follows:

"The law of the place where the parties have common habitual residence shall apply to essential validity of marriage; In the absence of such common habitual residence, the common national law of the parties shall apply; In the absence of both, the *lex loci celebrationis* shall apply provided that the marriage is celebrated in the place where one party has habitual residence or in the country of which one party has nationality."

The habitual residence and national law in China prevails over *lex loci celebrationis* which is the law to be applied for uncontested divorce, but divorce by litigation8, the *lex fori* shall apply.

Lex Patriae

As to adoption, the existing Chinese law, including the Adoption Act and the Measures of the Registration for Foreigners to Adopt Children in China, provides the conflict rules only in the situation where foreigners adopt children in China under which both adopters' *lex patriae* and Chinese law apply for the highest interest of the people of China and the children to be adopted taken into regard are the habitual residence of the adopter and adoptee and the *lex fori*.

Lex Loci Delicti

The law of the place where the wrong was committed in Common Law
lex loci protectionis and *lex loci delicti* are different from a doctrinal point of view, the practical outcome of the two approaches is largely similar. *lex loci protectionis* will be applied not only to infringement but also to ownership.
Lex loci delicti is the governing law for the Law of Torts in China and with *lex loci delicti* the two exceptions are: in the first place, if the alleged tort feasor and the victim have habitual residence in the same place, the law of that place shall apply and the law of the habitual residence of the parties replaces the *lex patriae* or the *lex domicilii* in this case. Parties involved can always choose the governing law after the event in issue, regional or international rules require an independent characterization which takes into account their regional or international nature.

All this is part of Consequentialism Jurisprudence where theories that assess acts character traits, practices, and institutions come into practice and the legal environment is tested according to the act that is most familiar with the consequences and a lot of policies are formulated in this manner. The moral act which is wrong is identified and the legal procedure that makes the moral wrong infused with legal implications is followed, then the penalties are decided accordingly. The test is that whether an act is right or wrong, the results are the deciding factor and the result is the judge of what is good or bad. If there is a benefit, then the result is good and if there is a loss or damage, then it is bad.

When choice of law overthrows vested rights this is where Freedom of Speech and Freedom of Expression as vested rights become a subject in Public Debates ad eventually in Consequentialism Jurisprudence. Ordinarily, these vested rights are highly regarded because of the articulation of opinions and ideas in the case of Freedom of Speech and there are legally permitted restrictions across the globe, showing that the rights are not absolute, although emergency situations are recognized as the only time when the freedom has to be suppressed. According to Justice Brandeis in Whitney v California (1927)Justia U S Supreme Court Center 274 U S 357,

'there should be more speech, not enforced suppression and only an emergency can justify repression…. Although the rights of free speech and assembly are fundamental, they are not absolute. Their exercise is subject to restriction when free speech would produce, a clear imminent danger of some substantive evil to society'

This may apply to many democracies, but alarmingly, such a title is not even a source of discussion in many sovereign nations because according to the latest UNESCO report on World Trends in Freedom of Expression and Media Development Global Report 2021/2022 there has been a decline by 85% of press freedom and many restrictions are being imposed. Collection of data from 160 countries has provided these key findings.

Data transmission has become even more restricted, media outlets are reducing in number, new laws and regulations are threatening Freedom of Expression and Press Freedom and sadly, Journalists are under attack and from 2016-2021 a total of 455 journalists have died on the job. Modern times have actually reduced the freedoms which are being disregarded in favor of security and most states can lawfully punish those who abuse these rights if there is any threat detected at all. This limitation by the government is very subjective to different sovereign states and control measures are usually seen through the application and issuance of permits, allowed meetings, political rallies and demonstrations with the content of speech fully controlled. Everything that goes outside the freedom is bound to find itself in copyright violation, trade mark suits, obscenity, sedition, incitement, libel, slander or any form of public order violation. This contains lawless behavior or any illegal conduct that would bring threats to business transactions, speech, intellectual property rights and every other act of any reasonable man within a context.

For the purpose of protecting human rights, territorial integrity (the borders of the state) or public safety, to prevent disorder or crime and to maintain morals and health, there is need to limit the Freedom of Speech. The Scandinavian countries and the Anglo sphere are doing extremely well in the influence and practice of free speech and the enjoyment of the right. There is limited, low or sometimes nonexistent support or any form of the Freedom of Speech in most Asian and the Arabic countries. The demand for Freedom of Speech in Africa is very high and a contrast in the picture of practice and support in many areas and the divergent support can be recorded in many countries.

Courtesy of V-Dem

Since democracy Burma/ Myanmar has improved, notably, Indonesia and Thailand are the highest. Laos is the lowest in Scores.

Some governments have been identified as distributing questionable information and the graph shows countries that have been accused of doctoring information especially in places where governments are less open to criticism. The power and ability for people to support high criticism of the government and its operations is highly supported in the Anglo sphere and Scandinavian countries, but showed a very high reluctance to talk about security matters.

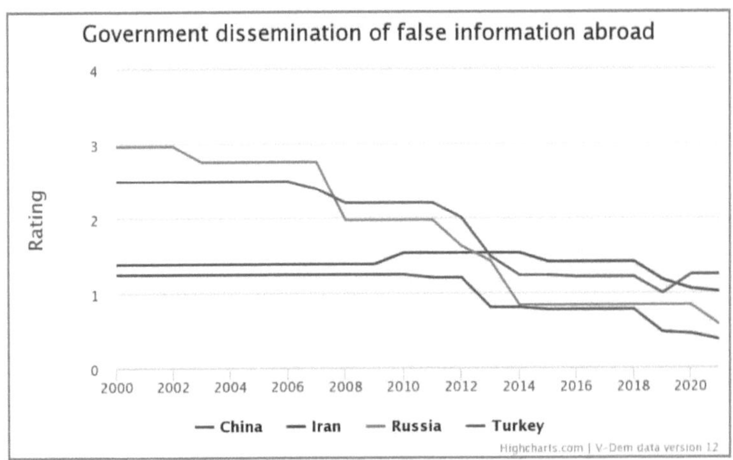

Courtesy of V Dem

There is a spread of disinformation with national security as a probable excuse and this has remained a challenge for many countries who fight for truth and democracy, but in whatever context it is taken, truth is seen as subjective and democracy is still considered as a political theory that is still exploring the application of norms and values at many different levels, the debate is continuous and very much in exhaustive, because the extension of politics is far and wide, but remember that private international rights also have a major role to play in many aspects of society. Legislative professionalism has been identified as one of the reasons for the global democratic deficit.

Repression tendencies of activities are well known in the Arab World and it goes with culture that the control measures are usually considered as excessive and arrests are many, recorded closures and dissolution of civic societies is not strange, but it must be remembered that these freedoms are only allowed in so far as their subjective countries allow.

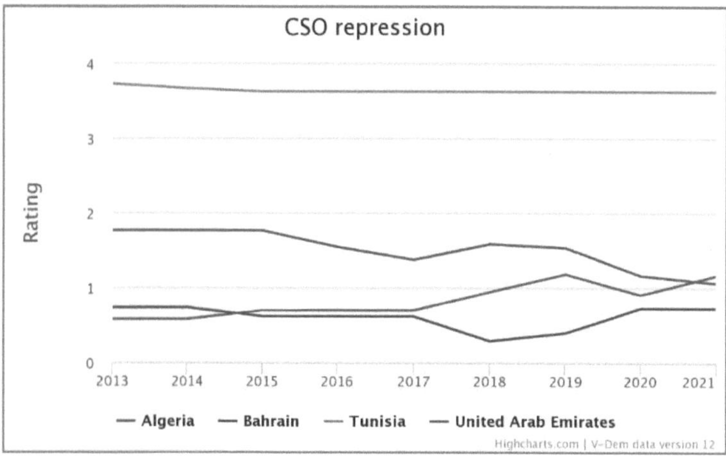

When it comes to ideas of social settings, access to services and enhancement of security, some governments take that into their custody as a measure of correction and control. And every political regime will usually come with its own ideals.

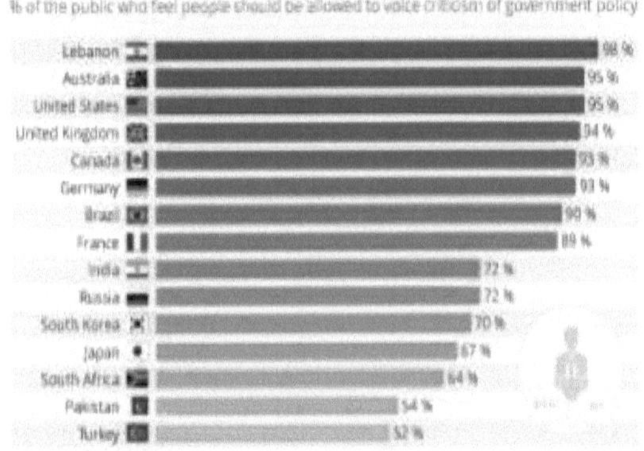

Courtesy of Statistica

Criticizing the government comes with the Freedom of Information and Transparency and both are a reflection of democracy because the government is made accountable for actions employed. On the flip side, democracy has been criticized as the cause of political instability, the debate is endless.

WORLD PRESS FREEDOM INDEX

INDIA SLIPS TWO PLACES

India made its debut on this index in 2013 at 140 out of 180 nations. The rankings gradually improved, reaching 136 in 2017. However, it has since slipped back to 140 this time. South Asia, in general, features poorly on the index, with Pakistan dropping three places to 142, and Bangladesh dropping four places to 150

Rank	Countries	Score	Rank	Countries	Score
1	Norway	7.82	10	Costa Rica	12.24
2	Finland	7.90	33	UK	22.23
3	Sweden	8.31	48	USA	25.69
4	Netherlands	8.63	106	Nepal	33.40
5	Denmark	9.87	140	**India**	45.67
6	Switzerland	10.52	142	Pakistan	45.83
7	New Zealand	10.75	149	Russia	50.31
8	Jamaica	11.13	150	Bangladesh	50.74
9	Belgium	12.07	177	China	78.92

This is interesting reading once again proving that the Scandinavian countries other than having a high approval of Freedom of Speech and Freedom of Expression, they also highly favor the Freedom of the press.

REFERENCES

1. Dr. Annabelle Bennett and Mr. Sam Granata (2019) When Private International Law Meets Intellectual Property Law: A Guide for Judges WIPO HCC
2. Justice Brandeis (2015) Freedom of Speech. Bureau Brandeis. Amsterdam. Netherlands

3. Zhengxin Huo (2011)Highlights of China's New Private International Law Act: From the Perspective of Comparative Law

CHAPTER FOUR

Controlling the Social Structures

The manner and form of communication will always matter because advanced methods of communication if unavailable will cause a discrepancy and problems for those without access. The behavior intention of those with a variety of media tools can be quickly observed by those who have access to social engagement and the exchange of information can command a social influence and opinions based on the information that will be passed. The control measures such as responses and outcome will show the level of influences that such engagement brings with the exchange of information. Depending on the influential that information is. The more influential the information, the more the interactions and as always, the influence of one individual is always less than the impact of for instance an industry with the same cause and Western Societies will always have enhanced views on any public debate. Public Opinion is enlarged by media expressions that will either integrate into new media or old media that will interact with the population and expression of opinions.

Opinions matter because they express a social environment and democracy is a core value of the United Nations and a lot more nations are championing the idea of democracy because there is representation from an elected government who have been decided by the citizens, but discontent is expressed in the political systems that enter with the garment of democracy and start practicing dictatorial tendencies in very subtle ways. The characteristics of democracy are expressed in elected representation, independence of the Judiciary, the vested rights or civil liberties, tolerance of each other by political factions and the exercise of the rule of law. Freedom of speech is one of the most important views of democracy.

At the Macro Level

This the broadest level and cuts between nations and across nations and examine global trends and changes. Communication skills at this at this level require the listener to understand, interpret and evaluate whatever is communicated and heard. The macro level skills are listening, speaking, writing and viewing, these are what are needed in successful communication hence the need for education even at the basic level that teaches these skills. The registration of conversations starts at this level when the basic rules are observed. Emotions will usually fall in this path in context or directive, depending on the function that is being followed. The object like macros, for example, codes, symbols and numeric fall in this path as well declaring a stimulation that takes no arguments because it is a sequence that follows a pattern. In the social context, at Macro level you look at institutions and these are the large scale patterns of communication that lead to globalization and the inter relationship between countries, at the Macro Level is where the laws and model laws that have been extensively discussed are categorized.

Uniformity

This usually happens when there is a shared background generally speaking, correspondence increases between the content on which communication networks and attitude-beliefs are defined, increasing group network connectivity is associated with increasing member uniformity.

Polarization: The dynamics that will influence extreme views on many issues are as a result of attitudes based on political influences, levels of tolerance, the availability of restrictions and norms that govern public behavior. Actions are usually done with a collective and the social groups often associated with an individual will affect the type of discussions and views that are likely to come out of asocial setting. The motive can also be derived from such an environment, before it is displayed as a form of behavior.

Clusterization

Speech is only valuable if it achieves its purpose that free speech has inherent value and is a right of autonomous moral agents, this is according to the theorists who advance nonconsenquentialism as opposed to consequentialism jurisprudence. In a cluster, **communication** range must cover itself and neighbor's **cluster**. A grid denotes a **cluster** the center position of a **cluster** is a centroid, that is, the average of all points and in terms of global influence, central is standardization and harmonization of data points, this is the central location of all points..

On a different level, the situation will be looked at as:

At Micro level

These interactions with the self when one is alone, interactions of a couple with one another or the interaction between friends within the social context by considering the social structures which may form the patterns of public opinion, this best applies on personal identities and balancing of multiple roles in society, this affects the communication style and transmission of messages. At this level studies show that work is more important to women, while leisure is very important to men.

The Meso Level

From one attracter to another this forms a network and the network will transition to other networks growing the wave of transition and the investigation of groups is at the Meso Level. This can be at work, in a sorority, at a club, a gang and how communication is transmitted and the organization of behavior patterns is subjective to what has impacted the group. At this level, what is more important is experience gained from interaction and perhaps a dependency on the social settings. Boundaries and balances are extremely influenced by the gate keepers and controllers of these social setting and hierarchy is determined or predetermined at this level.

One or all of these levels can help contain and control what will influence the publication or just the exchange of information by observing, analyzing and understanding what influences public opinion or the creation of the Court of Public Opinion. Public opinion many times is used as a means of control and a force to be used on an 'for or against' debate to control or sway public opinion and this is usually used by politicians or religions and this is one common factor of the two and many times, advocacy is birthed in this manner where the number of disagreements reduce and agreements increase inclined to an opinion tht will express itself as relevant to the society. If done in the correct way, various views can be obtained from opinion polls where questions are asked and answers are given and the views of the sample in a population are recorded and analyzed for research and recommendation purposes. In times of political campaigns this may be crucial, but when used to destroy a person or a personality, the effects can be very devastating.

The Court of Public Opinion is sometimes more influential because it has more people who may or may not even have th full understanding of the law who can sway the public into thinking anything that they hear, after the bulk of legal provisions that have been outlined, it is important to be cautious before forming any opinions.

REFERENCES;

1. James A Danowski (1980) Group Attitude Uniformity and Connectivity of Organizational Communication Networks for Production, Innovation, and Maintenance Content. International Communication Association. Oxford Academic. Oxford.
2. Ren Manfred, Andrea Guazzini, Carla Anne Roos, Tom Postmes and Namkje Koudenburgh (2020). Complejos. Spain.
3. Francisco J Leon Medina (2019) Endogenous Changes in Public Opinion. Journal of Artificial Societies and Social Simulation. Girona. Spain.

https://saylordotorg.github.io/text-priniples-of-sociology-

https://jcsites.juanita.edu

www.learnc.net

www.ibm.com

https://gcc.gnu.org

towardsdatascience.com.

CASES:

In *Boys v Chaplin* [1971] AC 356, the House of Lords recognised there could be an exception to this rule whereby a particular issue between the parties may be governed by the law that has the most significant relationship with the occurrence and the parties, leading in that case to displacement of the *lex loci*.

Morguard Investments Ltd v De Savoye [1990] SCR 1077. Canadian courts have adopted a more expansive approach, ruling that a real and substantial connection with the forum rendering the judgment is a sufficient basis for its recognition and enforcement

***Gulf Oil Corp. v. Gilbert*, 330 US 501 (1947) (US); *Spiliada Maritime Corp. v Cansulex Ltd* [1987] AC 460 (UK); *Wendell v Club Mediterranee NZ* [1989] 1 NZLR 216 (NZ).** A Court may deny jurisdiction if it concludes that another forum will be the most convenient and will best serve the interests of justice

Adams v Cape Industries plc [1990] Ch 433. A range of other connecting factors may also apply. Circumstances in which a judgment will be enforced at common law may include the following: (1) the judgment debtor was the plaintiff or counterclaimed in the proceedings; (2) the judgment debtor submitted to the jurisdiction of the foreign court by voluntarily appearing in the proceedings; (3) the judgment debtor had agreed to the jurisdiction of the forum with respect to the particular issue.

HUSTLER MAGAZINE, INC., ET AL. v. FALWELL no 86- 1278 U S Sepreme Court (1988) Petitioner Hustler Magazine, Inc., is a magazine of nationwide circulation. Respondent Jerry Falwell, a nationally known minister who has been active as a commentator on politics and public affairs, sued petitioner and its publisher, petitioner Larry Flynt, to recover damages for invasion of privacy, libel, and intentional infliction of emotional distress. The District Court directed a verdict against respondent on the privacy claim, and submitted the other two claims to a jury. The jury found for petitioners on the defamation claim, but found for respondent on the claim for intentional infliction of emotional distress and awarded damages. We now consider whether this award is consistent with the First and Fourteenth Amendments of the United States Constitution. HELD: We conclude that public figures and public officials may not recover for the tort of intentional infliction of emotional distress by reason of publications such as the one here at issue without showing in addition that the publication contains a false statement of fact which was made with "actual malice," *i. e.,* with knowledge that the statement was false or with reckless disregard as to whether or not it was true. This is not merely a "blind application" of the *New York Times* standard, see *Time, Inc.* v. *Hill,* 385 U. S. 374, 390 (1967), it reflects our considered judgment that such a standard is necessary to give adequate "breathing space" to the freedoms protected by the First Amendment.

57*57 Here it is clear that respondent Falwell is a "public figure" for purposes of First Amendment law.[5] The jury found against respondent on his libel claim when it decided that the Hustler ad parody could not "reasonably be understood as describing actual facts about [respondent] or actual events in which [he] participated." App. to Pet. for Cert. C1. The Court of Appeals interpreted the jury's finding to be that the ad parody "was not reasonably believable," and in accordance with our custom we accept this finding. Respondent is thus relegated to his claim for damages awarded by the jury for the intentional infliction of emotional distress by "outrageous" conduct. But for reasons heretofore stated this claim cannot, consistently with the First Amendment, form a basis for the award of damages when the conduct in question is the publication of a caricature such as the ad parody involved here. The judgment of the Court of Appeals is accordingly

Reversed.

JUSTICE KENNEDY took no part in the consideration or decision of this case.

JUSTICE WHITE, concurring in the judgment.

As I see it, the decision in *New York Times Co.* v. *Sullivan,* 376 U. S. 254 (1964), has little to do with this case, for here the jury found that the ad contained no assertion of fact. But I agree with the Court that the judgment below, which penalized the publication of the parody, cannot be squared with the First Amendment.

Printed by Books on Demand GmbH, Norderstedt / Germany